What do you think of the 21st century so far?

What do you think of the 21st century so far?

David Austin

**Guardian
Books**

For Janet

First published in 2004 by Guardian Books
Guardian Books in an imprint of Guardian Newspapers Ltd

A CIP record for this book is available from the British Library

ISBN 0 85265 051 5

Distributed by Politico's Publishing,
an imprint of Methuen Publishing Ltd,
215 Vauxhall Bridge Road, London SW1V 1EJ

Printed in Great Britain by Cambridge University Press

Cover Design: Two Associates
Text Design: www.carrstudio.co.uk

Contents

Introduction

Every working afternoon at the Guardian, after an hour or two pondering the news stories of the day, I draw nine little boxes and roughly sketch a cartoon idea in each of them. The editor of the day chooses one for the front page. Then the letters editor chooses another for the letters page.

They each pick the cartoon they find the funniest. As the funniest cartoon does not necessarily go with the day's most important story, the cartoons in this book are picked from an arbitrary selection.

Some things are hardly covered at all. European monetary policy, for instance, is not laughter material. There is nothing about the death of Diana or the September 11 attack. The emotional atmosphere after these events made it impossible for a pocket cartoonist to work.

This does not mean that the choice is restricted to the 'light-hearted' stories. I leave the building happiest when I have found a good joke about a serious subject.

Although this collection cannot claim to be a comprehensive history of the first few years of the third millennium, I hope that it reflects something of the experience of living through them. It is personal, biased and eccentric. A lot like any other history, in fact.

David Austin

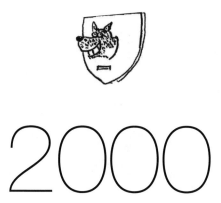

2000

January to March

2000

The new millennium got off to a disappointing start. The River of Fire didn't ignite. The dome's launch stranded its distinguished guests for hours on Stratford station. The Millennium Bridge wasn't ready and the Millennium Wheel wouldn't go round.

The Millennium bug also failed to precipitate the soothsayers' predicted electronic holocaust, but the flu bug crashed the NHS. BMW decided to sell the bits of Rover that it didn't want.

General Pinochet was too ill to stand trial and returned to Santiago and a miraculous recovery. Ken Livingstone was expelled from New Labour for daring to stand for Mayor of London. Frank Dobson was pushed unwillingly forward as the party's candidate. PY Gerbeau got that inverted poisoned chalice, the Dome.

The wrong kind of helicopter was sent to relieve floods in Mozambique. In Russia Mr Putin was elected to continue his Chechen war. Mr Haider, suspected of Nazi sympathies, was elected in Austria. President Clinton apologised for misleading the nation.

The Millennium Dome had begun to acquire its reputation as a disastrous failure from the very beginning. Celebrities had waited for hours on Stratford station to get to the millennium night launch party, They were offered compensation but they had to queue again to get it.

2000   Wednesday **January 12**

In the dome's first month it was 2 million visitors short of its over-optimistic predictions. It was decided to replace its director, Jenny Page. The headhunters entrusted with the job meant to bag the Disney executive Philippe Bourgignon but bagged his assistant, PY Gerbeau, instead.

Friday **February 11**   2000

PY was not the only foreigner risking unpopularity. Bavarian motor manufacturers BMW decided to sell off most of Rover, the last of the native car makers, which was collapsing under the weight of the overvalued pound.

2000   Thursday **March 16**

It was the anniversary of the MacPherson report into the Metropolitan police's handling of the inquiry into the murder of Stephen Lawrence and racial crime generally. It appeared that the Met was making slow progress in recruiting officers from ethnic minorities.

Thursday **February 24**

2000

In a move likely to find favour with some ethnic minority communities, the chief constable of Cleveland suggested that blanket prohibition of drugs was ineffective. He didn't see why possession of small quantities of cannabis should not be decriminalised.

2000   Thursday **February 17**

Doctors told Jack Straw that General Pinochet was suffering from senile decay and was too ill to be sent to Spain for trial. The tender-hearted home secretary let him go home to Chile instead.

Thursday January 13

2000

Sick citizens of this country stood to get less personal attention. In the interest of economy your 999 call might be redirected to NHS direct if judged not very urgent.

The Department of Trade and Industry's export credit guarantee system had backed loans to dubious governments to buy arms.

In Northern Ireland, the government once again threatened to impose direct rule and once again Mr Trimble threatened to resign. The unionists would not give an inch. The nationalists would not give up a single bullet.

2000   Friday **February 4**

2000

Ken Livingstone was elected Mayor of London. Frank Dobson was elected to The Wilderness. The Women's Institute slow hand-clapped Tony Blair for talking politics to them. In Northern Ireland the search for badges and uniforms for the reformed RUC that would offend nobody upset everybody. The IRA tried to cause traffic chaos by blowing up Hammersmith Bridge. The council closed the bridge and succeeded where the IRA had failed, The government contemplated banning foxhunting. Shooting burglars landed Tony Martin in jail and his victim in the cemetery. Not far away, hordes of chemical-warfare-suited Green protesters destroyed GM crops. Therapy and theology clashed over the issue of cloning. The public took a jaundiced view of NHS consultants' high-handed way with bits of their patients' dead bodies. Leo Blair was born, the first baby born to a serving prime minister for a very long time. Anarchists marched to Stop The City, but the collapse of dotcom share prices was far more effective in this respect, heralding the end of the long boom. Concorde crashed in flames near Paris, killing all the passengers and crew. The Russian submarine Kursk sank with all hands off Norway. The Dome struggled on, voraciously consuming money and reputations. Tate Modern opened. The Millennium Bridge opened, wobbled and closed again. The South African cricketer Hanse Kronje confessed tearfully to having taken bribes from a betting syndicate and England fans once again disgraced themselves on the continent.

Six-year-old Elian Gonzalez was rescued from the shipwreck in which his mother drowned, trying to flee Cuba. He was taken in by his expatriate great-uncle. Fellow expatriate Cubans made a political issue of his father's attempts to get him back. He became the object of a quasi-religious cult.

2000

Barclays Bank closed a swath of branches, leaving some 40,000 rural customers with no branch within reach. The bank had used some of the money saved to pay their new chief executive, Matthew Barrett, a great deal of money for his first three months' work.

Thursday **April 6**

2000

The Conservative party's treasurer and generous donor, Michael Ashcroft, was also a banker in Belize, the Caribbean tax haven. His participation in the colourful financial life of the region led to controversy when his peerage was proposed. This was exacerbated by his suggestion that he would sit as Lord Ashcroft of Belize.

2000

Monday **April 3**

Shares in dotcom and e-business companies, had boomed during the 1990s. Their value turned out to be only virtual.

Another enterprise conceived with great hope in the 1990s was the Millennium Dome. These hopes too were dashed in the new era. It was proving difficult to persuade people to visit the attraction.

2000 Tuesday **May 23**

Country folk fond of foxhunting were pleased to hear that Sir Terry Burns's inquiry into the rural pastime found no evidence that foxes pursued by hounds experienced 'pain and terror'.

Monday **May 22**

2000

The farmer Tony Martin shot intruder Fred Barras dead and wounded his fellow burglar. Despite approval of his actions in some quarters it seemed unlikely that this form of rural pest control would be legalised. Farmer Martin was sent to jail.

2000   Thursday **April 20**

The trade and industry secretary, Stephen Byers, spent £10 million on uneconomic collieries in old Labour areas of the midlands and the north-east. This was seen as an effort to establish friendly contact with the former owners of the party.

The government seemed to be losing touch with its new adherents too. Tony Blair was slow-hand-clapped by members of that bastion of middle England the Women's Institute. They objected to his talking politics to them.

2000 Thursday **June 18**

July to September

2000

The government presented a rather more human face when Euan Blair got drunk and Gordon Brown got married. William Hague tried to steal Euan's thunder with his claim to have consumed 14 pints of beer a day as a young man. The

royal family's standing momentarily improved as the Queen Mother celebrated her 100th birthday. Reality TV gripped the nation as viewers spied on people like themselves squabbling in the Big Brother house. ITV and the BBC also squabbled publicly over changing the times of the evening TV news broadcasts. Camelot looked like losing the lottery to Richard Branson. At the BBC Greg Dyke replaced John Birt and sacked a lot of people in suits. The government failed to repeal section 28 of the Local Government Act, which enjoined local government not to 'promote homosexuality'. Sexual offences were redefined. The News of the World published the addresses of paedophiles released from prison, setting off riots and the inevitable attack on a paediatrician. Sarah Payne's murderer was arrested. Lord Melchett of Greenpeace was acquitted of the charge of destroying GM crops. Reggie Kray died and had a traditional gangster's funeral. It was laughably suggested that hooligans should be marched to a cashpoint and fined on the spot. Adults began to be seen about town on tiny children's scooters. The government reported on itself and found that it had done very well. Protesters about fuel prices disagreed, bringing the government's popularity to a new low and the country nearly to a halt. Loyalist gangs began a turf war in Belfast. David Shayler, a dissident spy, spilled some secret service beans.

Britain imported a new TV phenomenon from Holland where it had proved to be both gripping and inexpensive. Viewers spied on people much like themselves locked into the Big Brother house, through the eyes of cameras placed in every room.

2000   Wednesday **July 19**

High fuel taxes, especially on diesel fuel for lorries, led to blockades of refineries and petrol stations. The Conservative party was quick to try to exploit this first real setback to the government's popularity.

Monday **September 18**   2000

Another widespread public concern was the fear of bovine spongiform encephalopathy, BSE. Research showed that the infection might spread from cattle to other species, including hamsters, recalling the Sun's famous contribution to news values.

Nato claimed that its bombing campaign in Kosovo was the most accurate ever. Experience on the ground suggested otherwise. Analysis showed that only 2% of unguided bombs and 40% of all bombs dropped by the RAF actually hit their target.

Wednesday August 16

2000

The EU was equally incompetent at bringing its good intentions to fruition. Aid sent to disaster areas was delayed by Brussels bureaucracy. Some shipments required 40 signatures before being dispatched. The South American victims of Hurricane Mitch and the subsequent floods had waited four years for relief.

2000   Monday **August 7**

A-levels may well have been getting easier to pass, but much more so for girls than for boys. They had been catching up on their male fellow pupils for a long time. This year they outperformed them in every category.

Friday **August 18**

2000

A group of academic economists proposed solving the universities' financial problems by charging up to £50,000 tuition fees. The failure of young males to get university places would not be an unmixed curse.

2000

The Home Office proposed a bill redefining sexual offences, to bear down more heavily on crimes considered heinous in our times, but legalising many activities offensive only to Victorian values. In particular it was no longer illegal for gay men to use public loos as trysting places.

Thursday July 27

2000

Paedophilia was a crime particularly prone to arouse public outrage. The News of the World decided to 'name and shame' paedophiles released from jail and living anonymously. The residents of the Paulsgrove estate in Portsmouth believed that they were living among them. They took their children along to the consequent riots, where they were seen shouting, 'Hang them!'

2000

Friday **August 11**

October to December

2000

The fuel tax protest fizzled out. A rail crash at Stevenage put pressure on Gerald Corbett of Railtrack to resign. Floods and storms caught the authorities unprepared. There was confusion over the replacement for the worn-out  Wembley stadium. Richard Desmond added the Daily Express and the Daily Star to his stable of pornographic publications. Who Wants to be a Millionaire did for ITV what Big Brother had done for Channel 4. The Enigma machine was stolen from Bletchley Park and inexplicably sent to the TV presenter Jeremy Paxman. There was controversy about the impending release of the murderers of James Bulger, who were then 18 years old. Another young child, Damilola Taylor, was murdered, probably by persons only a little older than himself. Robbers, using a JCB, failed to steal the Millennium Diamond from the dome. Chief schools inspector Chris Woodhead, scourge of the liberal educational establishment, resigned. Edward Heath retired. Michael Portillo came out as a liberal. He denied wanting to be leader. Geoffrey Robinson denied getting favours from the DTI. He didn't deny giving a million or so to Labour. There was controversy about the use of depleted uranium shells in Kosovo. The government proposed a Rapid Reaction Force to jet off to trouble spots. Bill Clinton's Middle-East summit failed to crown his presidency with success. A minority of Americans elected George W Bush president in a farcical election fought out mainly in the courts. A majority of Serbs removed Slobodan Milosevic from power. The legality of patenting human genes was disputed. The Nice summit was attacked by anti-globalisation protesters.

Ariel Sharon, leader of Likud, made a visit to the Temple Mount in Jerusalem and provoked, as he no doubt hoped and expected, a violent reaction from the Palestinians. They threw stones at Israeli tanks.

2000

Tuesday **October 3**

Reggie Kray died at 66. He had spent the first half of his life as a celebrity gangster and the second half in prison. He had a traditional East End gangster funeral attended by family, fellow criminals and the ageing celebrities he had known in his heyday.

Monday **October 2**

2000

Other gangsters who had achieved brief celebrity by trying to rob the dome went to jail. They had tried to steal a huge diamond from a display by De Beers by crashing in with a bulldozer and smoke bombs; instead they drove straight into a police trap.

2000

Tuesday **November 8**

Michael Portillo, the shadow chancellor, made a speech at the Tory party conference advocating tolerance of minorities, understanding and social inclusion. This was in contrast to his famous speech at a previous conference advocating the rather less liberal virtues of the SAS.

Friday **October 5**

2000

Another politician from the left of the Tory party, father of the house Sir Edward Heath, announced that he was to retire from parliament. He did not abandon his long sulky enmity with Lady Thatcher, the right-winger who had ousted him from the leadership.

Punching holes in their ballot papers was too confusing for many Florida voters. Some 19,000 papers were spoiled and an expected Democratic majority eliminated. This led to demands for recounts and a possible delay of several weeks before the result of the presidential election would be finally decided.

Ofsted inspector Chris Woodhead retired. This bugbear of the liberal educational establishment would doubtless have blamed teachers for the Florida voters' manual ineptitude. His retention by the Blair government had upset the teaching unions and most teachers celebrated his departure.

2000   Friday **November 3**

A law and order bill in the Queen's speech would propose that loutish behaviour should attract an on-the-spot fine, like a parking ticket. The government hoped it would stem a rising tide of yobbish behaviour. Those who would have to enforce it were less confident.

Thursday **December 7**

2000

Rising tides were not all metaphorical. England and Wales suffered flooding after fierce rainstorms. The deputy prime minister, John Prescott, promised initiatives to deal with global warming, which was naturally blamed for the bad weather, but seemed uncertain about what they might be.

2000   Wednesday **November 1**

2001

January to March

2001

Foot and mouth disease spread catastrophically from a ramshackle pig farm in Northumberland. The government's policy of containing it by killing and burning vast numbers of sheep and cattle upset the farmers. US tourists stayed away, allegedly believing that they might contract the disease. More realistically, they might fear getting deep vein thrombosis on the long transatlantic flight. Soldiers who had been in the Kosovo operation had fears about the effects of depleted uranium shells. A Libyan secret service man was jailed for the Lockerbie bombing. The Real IRA, die-hard dissenters from the peace process in Northern Ireland, bombed the BBC. Rail travel was dangerous. Even as Railtrack was trying to extricate itself from blame for the Hatfield crash there was another terrible accident at Selby. The dome's future was uncertain;

so was that of its champion, Peter Mandelson, who could not recall making a phone call supporting the passport applications of the Hinduja brothers, wanted for questioning in their native India. There were fears raised about other less wealthy persons seeking asylum. The Leicester MP Keith Vaz was less than forthcoming with Elizabeth Filkin, the Parliamentary Standards Commissioner. A general election date was due. There was speculation that Gordon Brown might use his considerable war chest for a pre-election give-away. Bill Clinton pardoned his brother, among others, as his last act as president. Ariel Sharon was elected in Israel. The war against the Chechen rebels grew even bloodier. The Taliban government of Afghanistan blew up two giant statues of the Buddha, which were offensive to their bleak fundamentalist creed.

American tourists were not coming to Britain, fearing they might catch foot and mouth disease. The tourist industry tried to persuade them that visits to urban Britain could be safe.

BSE and the foot and mouth epidemic gave the rest of the world the impression that the inhabitants of England and Wales were doomed and disease-ridden.

The animal inhabitants of these stricken countries were doomed. On English and Welsh farms thousands of sheep and cattle were shot and burned.

2001   Tuesday **March 27**

As the foot and mouth epidemic spread, vegetarians, already free of guilt, could feel safe as well.

Unlike vegetarians, the directors of Balfour Beatty, the firm responsible for maintaining the railway track at Hatfield, could not feel guilt-free. They had known about the cracked rail that led to the fatal crash for at least 10 months but had done nothing.

Gary Hart, whose Land Rover caused a rail disaster at Selby, was charged with causing the deaths of 10 passengers. This was the third rail disaster in England in 18 months.

Monday **March 12**

2001

58

Not only Britain's railways required attention. The NHS was in a pretty run-down state as well. The chancellor, Gordon Brown, suggested that people might volunteer to help out. This would foster community spirit as well as save money.

2001 Friday **January 12**

The lord chancellor, Derry Irvine, had raised funds for Labour from barristers, whose leader he was. When criticised for this he decided that he had done nothing wrong and thus had nothing to apologise for.

Following the recommendations of the report into the murder of Stephen Lawrence, the Metropolitan police claimed success in recruiting ethnic minorities. It turned out, however, that they had counted white Irish, Australian and Canadian recruits, which was not at all what was intended. In fact they had only four new black policemen.

2001

April to June

2001

After some shilly-shallying Tony Blair fixed the date of the election as June 7. The Tories fell out over the issue of race. Things livened up a little when John Prescott punched a heckler but apathy was the government's main opponent. It claimed plenty of votes, but Labour won. William Hague fell and the fight over the Tory succession, which had begun well before the election, got going in earnest. There was controversy about whether to control foot and mouth disease by culling or vaccination. Phoenix, the calf who escaped the flames, was produced in evidence for vaccination. On May Day police impounded a mixed bag of shoppers and rioters in Oxford Street for a very long time. There were race riots in Oldham. A lorry driver was jailed for 14 years for allowing the people he was smuggling into the country to suffocate, Hanse Kronje gave evidence about corruption in cricket. Lord Archer went on trial for perjury. Ronnie Biggs the Great Train

Robber came back from Brazil and went straight back to jail. The Cullen report on the Great Train Crashers was published. Lambeth police experimented with tolerating cannabis. A Chinese fighter buzzed an American spy plane too enthusiastically and collided with it. The spy plane came down on a Chinese island, provoking diplomatic exchanges and a very thorough search by the Chinese. President Bush revived Star Wars as 'National Missile Defense' and invited the British to help him at Fylingdales and Menwith. President Kostunice of Serbia was under pressure to send the ex- president Milosevic to The Hague. Israel responded to Palestinian attacks by assassinating activists and full-scale attacks on Gaza using F-16s' thereby upsetting the Americans. In Africa suspected child slaves vanished from a ship off the coast. Drugs companies were attacked for not making AIDS drugs cheaply available. Crops failed in Zimbabwe.

Scotland Yard, fed up with drugs busts that involve reams of paperwork and lead to a £10 fine in the magistrates' court, decided to relax its attitude to cannabis. Starting in Lambeth, people possessing the drug would only be cautioned. Hardliners said the police were going soft.

2001   Friday **June 15**

Recent spectacular progress in genetic science had not yet been brought to bear on the epidemic of foot and mouth disease. Killing and burning the animals that might carry the disease was a gruelling and grisly task for many hundreds of people.

Friday **April 6**

2001

The many hundreds involved in the mass slaughter might well have been recruited from those who formerly worked in tourism. Tourists were still unwilling to visit what was represented in the media as a vast open-air slaughterhouse. Others were alleged to believe that they might fall victim to the disease themselves.

Ronnie Biggs the Great Train Robber returned from 35 years of exile in Brazil, where he had fled after escaping from prison. He took up his long prison sentence where he had left off, in Belmarsh jail.

Tuesday **May 8**

2001

Unlike the returned felon, immigrants were not welcomed to Britain. When they did manage to get in they were exploited by unscrupulous employers to do the jobs that no British wanted.

2001   Thursday **April 26**

Anti-globalisation rioters disrupted the meeting of the European Union leaders at Gothenburg. They reacted with extreme violence.

Monday **June 18**

2001

In the election campaign Conservative politicians had painted a picture of extreme violence much closer to home. Under Labour's lax rule, they said, our streets were the playground of criminals, bent on destroying the respectable.

2001   Thursday **May 17**

The Conservatives' election manifesto promised not cuts in income tax but 6p a litre cut in petrol tax. They hoped thus to take advantage of the recent protests about high fuel prices.

Friday **May 11**

2001

The Conservatives never got back the money they spent on fuel for their battle buses. Labour won the election, but both parties had spent (by British standards) huge amounts on the campaign. Both were short of cash.

July to September

2001

Reality TV reached new depths or profundity, according to your point of view, with a show based on the trenches in the first world war. The battle for the Tory leadership was characterised by bungling and ill humour. Bradford exploded in violent race riots. In Colombia three IRA men  were arrested, charged with training the local FARC terrorists. General De Chastelain said that the IRA at home was sticking to its guns. Mr Trimble walked out of the devolved assembly. The children of the Holy Cross Catholic primary school were attacked by Loyalist mobs. Ken Livingstone and Bob Kiley lost their legal battle with the government to prevent the private financing of the tube. The economy continued its slow decline. In Israel Ariel Sharon's policy of confrontation continued. Anti-globalisation protesters rioted in Genoa. The Yugoslav civil war threatened to break out again in Macedonia. Slobodan Milosevic would not recognise the court at The Hague. The attack on the World Trade Centre on September 11 led to President Bush's War on Terror and more immediately to his war on the Taliban government of Afghanistan. Attitudes hardened enough to delight the hard heart of Osama bin Laden himself. It was a horrible three months.

Tony Blair and Taioseach Bertie Ahern set Monday August 6 as a take-it-or-leave-it deadline to break a deadlock in negotiations over the peace process initiated by the Good Friday agreement. It seemed most probable that all parties would leave it.

2001

Thursday **August 2**

The health secretary, Alan Milburn, announced that NHS patients would be able to have their operations in other EU countries with better-provided health services. This would serve to shorten hospital waiting lists as promised by the government.

Monday **August 27**

2001

The government believed that many other allegedly sick persons were feigning incapacity as a way of inflating their unemployment benefits. It was proposed to keep a strict eye on them. Labour backbenchers threatened rebellion.

Thursday **July 5**

The Home Office announced that the police were only solving 24 per cent of all recorded crime.

Thursday **July 19**

2001

Public passions were aroused more by paedophilia than burglary. The
suspicion that paedophiles released from prison were being housed there
had led to fierce riots on the Paulsgrove estate in Portsmouth. The Channel 4
spoof documentary series Brass Eye satirised the panic and upset not only
the people of Paulsgrove but also culture secretary, Tessa Jowell.

2001

The industrial powers had met in Bonn to debate the Kyoto protocol on the use of fossil fuels. It was agreed that one way for nations unable to restrain their desire to burn oil could compensate for it was to grow trees to mop up the resultant carbon dioxide.

Tuesday **July 24**

2001

Falling profits and fear of approaching recession did not motivate British executives to restrain their desire to award themselves massive pay increases. They gave themselves an average rise of 28 per cent, compared to last year's relatively modest 16 per cent.

2001   Wednesday **August 29**

The parents of Catholic schoolchildren asserted their right to walk to Holy Cross primary school in North Belfast along a road bordered by Protestant houses. Protestants responded by hurling stones, bombs and abuse at them. Police trying to keep the two sides apart were injured. Neither side appeared ready to take seriously the injunction of their religion's founder to love one another.

Tuesday **September 4**   2001

Tolerance between Christians and Muslims was also under strain after the attacks on the World Trade Centre by declared Muslim fundamentalists. Silvio Berlusconi, the Christian media magnate turned prime minister of Italy, enthusiastically expressed the view that his civilisation was inherently superior to theirs. Few, however, would claim that his TV channels occupied the commanding heights of culture.

2001   Thursday **September 27**

October to December

2001

Osama bin Laden's organisation, al-Qaida, was identified as the enemy responsible for the September 11 attack. The US waged war on Afghanistan, al-Qaida's refuge, mostly from the air. Tony Blair was the president's most enthusiastic ally. Kabul and Kandahar were soon taken. Bin Laden 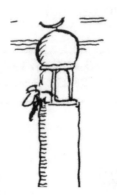 slipped away from the caves of Tora Bora unobserved by the warlord allies of the US and the British SAS. Mullah Omar made his escape on a motor bike. Homeland security went onto a war footing. The curtailed Labour party conference was ringed with steel. It was completely dominated by the prime minister, who was now a great figure on the world stage. There were scares about letters containing anthrax powder. Asylum seekers had to carry identity cards and could be summarily interned. The chancellor of the exchequer remained resolutely optimistic about the economy, but the long slide continued. So did the troubles of the railways. The transport minister, Stephen Byers, got into trouble trying to sort them out. The Provisional IRA, perhaps feeling that al-Qaida had given terrorism a bad name, eschewed the armed struggle. The Real IRA had no such scruples. The escapist fantasies of Harry Potter and The Lord of the Rings were unsurprisingly popular. The struggle in Israel and Palestine continued with murder and counter murder. Chairman Arafat's office was besieged. In Greece some British plane spotters were arrested on suspicion of spying. Another British eccentric, Richard Reid, was arrested in the act of trying to blow up an airliner by exploding his own trainers.

The attack on the Taliban government had so far been carried out by aircraft high above Afghanistan. They bombed anti-aircraft defences, radar, the few aircraft owned by the regime and any of the unshaven enemy they could spot.

The al-Jazeera TV station broadcast a video that purported to have been made by Osama bin Laden. In it he threatened another attack on a tall building.

Monday **October 15**

2001

Bin laden was also suspected of being responsible for posting the letters containing anthrax powder that had caused terror in the US.

2001 Monday **October 22**

David Blunkett, the home secretary, proposed that immigrants to this country should attend citizenship classes, to learn British values and the English language. They might also revive lost civilities.

The home secretary would not want Immigrants to acquire the British aversion to carrying identity cards. In order to get state support, asylum seekers would have to carry smart cards, replacing the 'humiliating' voucher system.

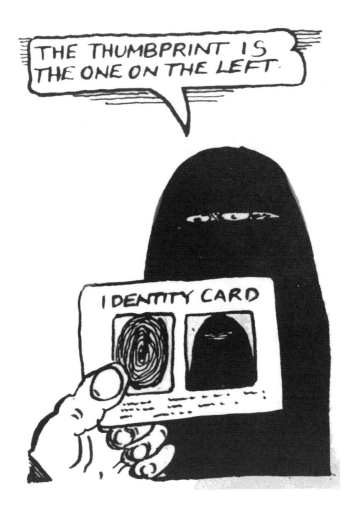

2001   Friday **October 26**

The government proposed legislation to compel separated parents to allow estranged partners, mostly fathers, access to the children.

Monday **October 29**

2001

It seemed that the law did not offer sufficient protection to clergymen threatened by violent parishioners. They were offered martial arts training; should turning the other cheek prove ineffective.

2001   Monday **December 17**

David Blunkett, the home secretary, announced that he intended to downgrade cannabis from a class B to a class C drug, no more dangerous, perhaps, than alcohol or tobacco. It seemed that it might be on the way to being legalised.

Wednesday **October 24**

2001

British life was changing in other ways. A report on the riots in Bradford, Burnley and Oldham during the summer initiated a debate on race relations. David Blunkett's contribution was to urge immigrants to integrate.

2001   Tuesday **December 11**

2002

January to March

2002

Tony Blair spent much of the time abroad, in his new role as deputy world leader. He took a holiday in Egypt, negotiated for peace between India and Pakistan and promised to sort out Africa's problems for the Africans. At home much trouble was brewing. Businessman Lakshmi Mittal, who had given money to Labour, had been offered cheap EU loans, which he used to set up Romanian competition to the British steel industry. BAe tried to sell an over-expensive air traffic control system to Tanzania. At home, our own new ATC system kept breaking down. Spin-doctor Jo Moore was in trouble for urging government departments to release bad news under the cover of the September 11 outrage. She then rowed publicly with Martin Sixsmith, Stephen Byers's press officer. The government was forced to pay off shareholders in the failed Railtrack before it could set up Network Rail in its place. The privatised examiner Edexcel failed to print A-level papers correctly. The dome failed to get sold. The Whittington Hospital failed to find a bed for an old lady and also failed to keep the fact out of the press. social services had failed to protect young Victoria Climbié from her murderers. ITV Digital failed. Despite all these failures Tony Blair's popularity held up. There was a scare that the MMR triple injection caused autism. The Lambeth police chief, Brian Paddick confessed online to a sympathy for anarchism. Police Chief Ronnie Flanagan denied failing to heed warnings about the Omagh bomb. Prince Harry went on a drink and drugs education course. Enron crashed spectacularly, bringing down the Press Complaints Commission head, Lord Wakeham, with it. President Bush evaded blame for his own involvement. He then choked on a pretzel. His administration said that it planned to attack Iraq. The general election in Zimbabwe was stitched up in Robert Mugabe's favour. The Queen Mother died, aged 101.

Having rather quickly ousted the Taliban regime from Afghanistan, the Bush administration was said to be planning to attack Iraq, with the intention of ousting Saddam Hussein.

High in the skies, the US forces were unable to detect their defeated enemies slinking away from Afghanistan along routes pioneered by drug smugglers.

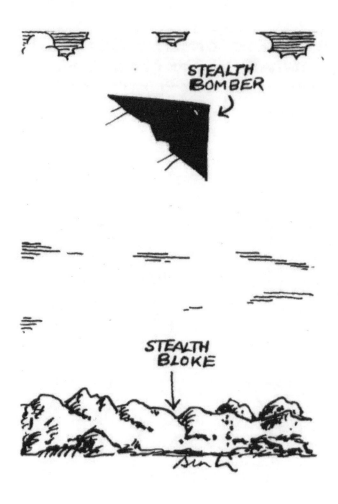

The Talibs and fellow travellers who were caught were taken to Camp X-Ray at Guantánamo Bay. There, as enemies of freedom, they were locked away from the rest of the world in manacles, leg irons and bright orange overalls.

2002

Monday January 21

We hoped that the threat of terrorist attack had made security extremely stringent. It was therefore rather alarming when thieves easily evaded Heathrow's security to steal $6.5 million in transit from Bahrain to New York.

Tuesday **February 12**

2002

No security forces were present when President Bush was watching the Miami Dolphins play the Baltimore Ravens on TV. He attempted to eat a pretzel at the same time. The task was beyond him and he choked, losing consciousness for a short time. His enemies took note.

Tony Blair had visited Egypt, India, Pakistan and Afghanistan in his new role as assistant world statesman.

Tuesday **January 8**

2002

While the prime minister was otherwise engaged his underlings had been misbehaving. Jo Moore, the government spin-doctor had to resign over her alleged bullying of civil servants. She was already in trouble for describing September 11 as 'a good day to bury bad news'. A fierce row with her fellow press officer Martin Sixsmith brought her career to an end.

2002

Friday **March 1**

President Mugabe had put the army in charge of the presidential election. Few Zimbabweans expected them to be impartial. The conclusion of the election was looking very much foregone.

Monday **March 4**

Not having President Mugabe's command of the media, ITV's digital TV venture also came to a conclusion. Its only successful element had been the knitted monkey doll used to promote it.

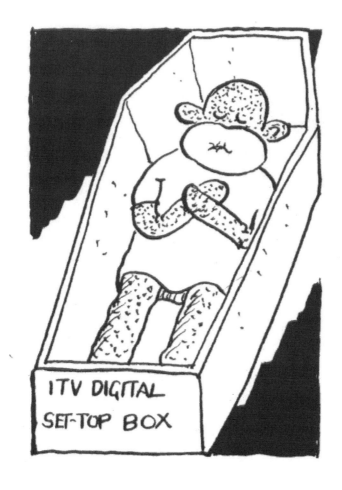

2002

April to June

2002

Mothers generally were threatened with losing benefits if their children misbehaved. One mother in particular was jailed for failing to send her child to school. The Queen Mother was more honoured. People queued for hours to file past her coffin. The transport secretary, Stephen Byers, resigned his unenviable job. Network Rail replaced Railtrack. Powderject landed the disputed contract for smallpox vaccine. This was said to be unconnected with their donation to the Labour party. Yarlswood camp for asylum seekers burned down. The stock market continued to fall, dragging down pension funds with it. The alleged murderers of Damilola Taylor were not convicted. Brazil beat England in the semi-final of the World Cup. The national lottery, beginning to flag, was re-branded. A man dressed as a monkey was elected Mayor of

LADY THATCHER

Hartlepool. Mayor Livingstone denied being in a drunken brawl at a party. The Dutch government fell because of its troops' failure at Srebrenice. The Dutch general election candidate Pym Fortuyn was assassinated. His new party subsequently came second. M Le Pen beat Lionel Jospin into third place, forcing many people to vote for M Chirac, some holding their noses as they did so. Ariel Sharon's army invaded Yasser Arafat's compound. Palestinians responded with more suicide bombings. A group of activists were besieged in the Church of the Nativity in Bethlehem. President Bush sent Secretary of State Powell to the Middle East. He did not achieve anything. Neither did the Royal Marines and Afghan warlords who searched caves in Afghanistan. War between India and Pakistan seemed probable. So did war between the USA and Iraq.

The nation's absorption in the Queen Mother's funeral arrangements might provide the sort of cover provided (in spin-doctor Jo Moore's view) by the events of September 11.

2002   Monday **April 1**

There were shocked complaints that a BBC newsreader had not worn a black tie while announcing the Queen Mother's death.

Other mothers attracted less sympathetic attention. Those unable to prevent their offspring committing crimes stood to lose their social security benefits.

2002

The US decided to share its missile defence technology, the enormously expensive Strategic Defence Initiative, with Russia, recalling the white elephants given by Siamese emperors to unfortunate subjects.

Thursday **May 16**   2002

Another unwelcome offer from the US was the advice offered to the Israeli government. The president suggested 'as a friend' that Israel should withdraw from the Palestinian cities it had recently occupied.

2002   Monday **April 8**

England lost 2-1 to Brazil in the World Cup, but Tim Henman was not yet out of Wimbledon.

England's professional demonstrating team, with a few foreign players, played the police on May Day. The disturbances were small but thoroughly professional on both sides and resulted in a no-score draw.

2002

Thursday **May 2**

Lady Thatcher, the former prime minister, was honoured by Parliament. The members commissioned a statue from the sculptor Neil Simmonds. It was unveiled in the Guildhall.

Wednesday **May 22**

2002

The Labour party was rather less honoured. It accepted a donation from Richard Desmond, who had become proprietor of the Daily Express using the profits from his pornographic magazines.

2002   Monday **May 13**

July to September

2002

House prices went on rising as stock markets went on falling worldwide. The chancellor opted for more tax and more spending to improve 'bog standard' schools and the NHS. There was controversy about falling A-level standards and inaccurate marking. Teachers were checked for paedophilia, very slowly. Brazil beat England in the semi-finals of the World Cup. The Commonwealth games were a modest success. The FA lost money in the crash of ITV Digital and the head of ITV lost his job. Romeo Beckham was born. Nicholas van Hoogstraten went to jail. So did two of the men cleared of murdering Stephen Lawrence, for racially abusing a black policeman. Two people were arrested for the abduction and murder of two young girls in Soham. The drugs taar resigned. Leftwinger Derek Simpson was elected to head Amicus. The Labour party was short of money. Ken Livingstone failed to rejoin it. Rowan Williams was to be the new Archbishop of Canterbury. The

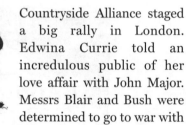

Countryside Alliance staged a big rally in London. Edwina Currie told an incredulous public of her love affair with John Major. Messrs Blair and Bush were determined to go to war with Iraq, but the rest of us were at best lukewarm in our support. The US bombed an Afghan wedding party. An Afghan family were evicted from a British mosque and sent to Germany. Australia returned to its penal roots in its treatment of Afghan refugees. Europe wrangled over the CAP, Spain and Morocco wrangled over tiny Parsley Island off the latter's coast. Negligent air traffic control and misunderstanding between ATC and a Russian pilot caused a collision over Switzerland. President Bush and Vice President Cheney were both accused of dubious financial practices. Nine miners were miraculously rescued from a flooded pit in Pennsylvania. The Greens helped Chancellor Gerhard Schröeder scrape back into power.

Fire-fighters were about to hold a special conference to decide on an all-out strike. It was widely believed that the government had already decided to go to war in Iraq. The army would be called on to participate in both crises.

2002

The Lambeth experiment, downgrading cannabis to a class C drug, was judged to be a success. David Blunkett announced that the policy was to be adopted countrywide, with a beneficial effect on crime statistics.

Wednesday **July 10**

2002

It was not thought advisable to massage the statistics by legalising hooliganism. The government proposed instead to discourage yobs by fining them on the spot, like illegal parkers.

2002

Mr Tebbit had famously declared that nationality determined which team you cheered on. For the World Cup final, supporters of the England national team switched their allegiance to Brazil, who had beaten them in the semi-final.

Monday **July 1**

2002

The former international footballer George Best had famously led a life devoted to wine, women and song. The first of these had destroyed his liver. He had a replacement transplanted at the Cromwell Hospital.

2002

Wednesday **July 31**

The government refused to pay for Michael Meacher to go to the Johannesburg Earth Summit. Alastair Campbell said that they wanted to cut down on ministerial 'junkets'. Green pressure groups believed that the real reason was that Mr Meacher was too sympathetic to their cause and offered to pay his air fare.

SAVE
THE
MEACHER

President Bush said that he modelled himself on Winston Churchill.

Thursday **August 29**

The Countryside Alliance was an organisation of middle-class country folk. It was formed in response to the government's stated intention to ban foxhunting with hounds. It had organised a highly successful demonstration in London.

Friday **September 27**

2002

Philandering was another sport that entered the political arena. Edwina Currie wrote about her eroto-comic love affair with John Major, which had enlivened a few party conferences.

October to December

2002

President Clinton was more popular with the delegates than the Prime Minister at the Labour conference. Iain Duncan Smith told the Tory Conference not to underestimate a quiet man, but they continued to do so. A Republican spy was discovered in the Northern Ireland Chief Executive's office. The assembly collapsed. Fire fighters started a long strike. Education Secretary Estelle Morris resigned under pressure, mostly from the press. The Queen intervened to stop the trial for theft of Burrell, Princess Diana's butler. Lord Archer published his prison diaries. David Shayler, the whistle blowing spook, was not allowed a public interest defence and got 6 months in jail. Peter Foster helped Cherie Blair buy a couple of flats in Bristol. He turned out to be a convicted con man.

The refuge for asylum seekers at Sangatte, near Calais, closed. UN inspector Hans Blix returned to Iraq. Mr Bush's party did quite well in the mid-term elections. Mr Blair fell out with President Chirac over EU enlargement and the CAP. The Spanish navy illegally stopped a North Korean ship delivering weapons to Yemen. Two snipers terrorised the area around Washington DC. Several states competed for the right to try, and subsequently execute, them. The Catholic Church in the USA was engulfed in a child abuse scandal. Terrorists exploded a car bomb outside a night club in Bali, killing many people. Chechen terrorists took hostages in a Moscow theatre. The siege was brought to a bloody end by security forces. Riots forced the Miss World competition out of Nigeria

President Clinton excited the Labour party conference with an outstanding speech. Mrs Currie had excited the Tory conference with her bedroom confessions, an area in which the president was well known to take an interest.

2002   Thursday **October 3**

A Slough magistrate fined Princess Anne £500 for allowing her bull terrier Dottie to bite two boys in Windsor Great Park. The Queen did not intervene, as she had in the case of Paul Burrell, the former butler accused of stealing from the late Princess Diana.

The crown court judge, Cherie Blair, had gained a reputation for new-age dottiness from revelations about her dealings with 'style guru' Carole Caplin.

2002   Tuesday **December 10**

As fire-fighters went on strike for the first time in 25 years, the army, with very little experience of the kind of thing fire-fighters do, prepared to provide emergency cover.

In view of the army's inexperience, while fire-fighters were on strike people refrained from activities that might require their services.

Friday **November 15**

Pension funds were running out of money. The work and pensions secretary, Andrew Smith, proposed that we should solve the problem by working on after retirement age until we either had saved enough or died.

The lifestyles of younger folk were also changing. The Lords voted in a law allowing gay couples to adopt children. The Tory leader, Iain Duncan Smith, had opposed the measure with a three-line whip in the Commons. This had made him unpopular with some Tories, popular with others.

2002

Saddam Hussein's government sent the UN a huge pile of papers containing information about his country's efforts to make nuclear and other weapons. It seemed possible that by the time it had all been read it would be too late to attack him.

Tuesday **December 10**

2002

Joe Gormley, the miners' leader in the strike that brought down the Heath government in the early 1970s, had also been supplying information. Union members were surprised to learn that he had been supplying it to Special Branch MI5.

2002   Thursday **October 24**

2003

January to March

2003

A congestion charge was introduced in central London. A short snowfall brought traffic in the south-east of England to a halt. Two young women were killed in the crossfire of a gang fight in Birmingham and gun wielding farmer Tony Martin was refused parole. Dolly, the cloned sheep, died aged 6 and was stuffed. Rowan Williams was enthroned as Archbishop of Canterbury.

American and British forces moved to the Gulf in preparation for war in Iraq. Tony Blair tried to get another resolution in the UN, to back up resolution 1441. France, Germany and Russia frustrated him. On March 20 the war started anyway. There was an anti-terror exercise in the City of London. 304 people were arrested as possible terrorists and 3 charged. Perhaps inspired by these events

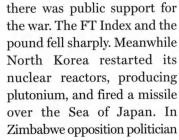

there was public support for the war. The FT Index and the pound fell sharply. Meanwhile North Korea restarted its nuclear reactors, producing plutonium, and fired a missile over the Sea of Japan. In Zimbabwe opposition politician Morgan Tsvangirai went on trial, President Mugabe went to France at the request of the French government and the England cricketers did not go to play there. The match was played in South Africa where some brave Zimbabwean players wore black armbands to mourn the loss of decent government in their country. The shuttle Columbia broke up high over the USA. In Northern Ireland the IRA were unwilling to declare the war over and elections were postponed. In Israel terror and counter terror, in abeyance since last November, resumed.

Tony Blair had told parliament that there was a moral case for the war, to remove Saddam's oppressive regime. He had also said that Saddam could stay in power if only he gave up his weapons of mass destruction. Then, of course, there was the war on terrorism.

2003   Wednesday **February 26**

Weapons inspectors had found an Iraqi rocket with a range slightly longer than is permitted by the UN. The Iraqis obligingly modified it on the spot to shorten its range.

The coalition forces, at last fighting their way to Baghdad, had more to consider than Saddam's weapons. They must win the hearts and minds of the Iraqi people, pointing out the benefits to be had from the west.

2003   Friday **March 28**

Andrew Motion, the poet laureate, wrote a 30-word poem attacking President Bush's, and Her Majesty's government, policy towards Iraq.

The news media too were being uncooperative. The BBC was thought to be anti-war. Iraqi TV viewers saw pictures of American prisoners, relayed by al-Jazeera.

2003   Monday **March 24**

The new archbishop, Rowan Williams, was enthroned. He had upset the prime minister by rubbishing his moral case for the war in Iraq.

Friday **February 28**

2003

The impending war had resulted in an unusual harmony of opinion among the British.

The Government Skills Agency reported that British 5 year-olds lacked 'basic communication skills' and could not speak audibly, listen or recite nursery rhymes when they arrived at school.

Those 5-year-olds who finally develop enough communication skills to get to university will have to pay their way while there with a huge loan, and the posher the university the bigger the loan.

2003

It was a very hot summer. Clare Short finally resigned from the front bench. George Galloway MP was banned from all office in the party. The government came into conflict with the BBC over journalist Andrew Gilligan's claim that 'an official'  had told him that the dossier on Iraq's weapons of mass destruction (WMDs) had been 'sexed up'. In his budget statement the Chancellor had to announce that he had been too optimistic about growth. Some schools actually ran out of money and had to sack staff. The Tory party continued to quarrel over Iain Duncan Smith's leadership. Labour did well enough in local and regional elections. The office of Lord Chancellor was abolished, upsetting some judges. Mr Bush visited Northern Ireland. He told the inhabitants to stop fighting and disarm. The IRA responded ambiguously and elections were postponed. President Putin of Russia made a state visit to Britain. A cull of hedgehogs on the island of Uist upset animal lovers. Severe Acute Respiratory Syndrome, SARS, added to the terrors of international travel.

President Bush declared 'mission accomplished' in Iraq in May. The Iraqi people at first celebrated their new-found freedom by rioting, looting and fighting. Giscard d'Estaing proposed a constitution for the European Union. Suicide bombers attacked American targets in Saudi Arabia. Poland and Lithuania voted to join the EU. A Russian Soyuz rescued three astronauts marooned in the International Space Station by the destruction of the shuttle Columbia. Tribal fighting led to massacres in the Congo. The opposition took a sceptical view of President Obasanjo's election victory.

Alastair Campbell, the prime minister's press secretary, accused the BBC of lying. The BBC correspondent Andrew Gilligan had claimed on the Today programme that dossiers the government prepared to make the case for war with Iraq had exaggerated information from the security services.

The American forces had issued a special pack of cards portraying the 55 most wanted member of the Saddam regime. Despite their best efforts they were unable to spot the Ace of Spades, the dictator himself.

Equally elusive were the weapons of mass destruction advanced by the government as the chief reason for making war on Iraq. They began to seem like a fairy tale.

Monday **June 2**

The US general Tommy Franks called together the Iraqi politicians chosen by the defence secretary, Paul Wolfowitz, and discussed the finer points of democracy with them.

It is not clear how much the general emphasised the role business plays in western democracy. It seemed possible that US companies might turn out to be more equal than others when it came to sharing out contracts to rebuild the country.

New Hampshire announced that it intended to appoint an openly gay man as bishop. The gay canon Jeffrey John was destined to become bishop of Reading. This provoked a furious reaction from conservative elements in the Church of England.

There was disharmony too in New Labour. It was widely believed that at the famous Granita lunch Mr Blair had promised to yield his place to the chancellor. Mr Blair's fiftieth birthday seemed like a good time to deliver on that promise.

2003

France had enraged the US by refusing to back the war in Iraq. This had led the chef at the House of Representatives' restaurant to rename French fries as freedom fries. Eurosceptics were enraged by Giscard d'Estaing's proposed EU constitution.

Tuesday **May 27**

2003

Eurosceptics felt that Giscard d'Estaing's proposed EU constitution would lead to Europe becoming a federal super-state. Federal had become a dirty word among them.

2003   Wednesday **May 28**

July to September

2003

Dr David Kelly a former arms inspector in Iraq who had spoken to the BBC's correspondent Andrew Gilligan was found dead in the woods, apparently having killed himself. The Prime Minister set up an inquiry under Lord Hutton to examine the circumstances. Communications director Alastair Campbell resigned, although allegedly not because of these events. At home the government ran into trouble with the Lords over foxhunting and with its back-benchers over jury trials and 'foundation' hospitals. The Liberal Democrats won Brent East. The Chancellor, Gordon Brown, seemed to back Old Labour at the annual conference. Tony Blair went on an overseas tour. The Eurostar link between Folkestone and the outskirts of London opened. A gay man became Bishop of New Hampshire but the Church of England, fearing schism, prevented Canon Jeffrey John from accepting the see of Reading. Lord Archer was released from jail having served two of his four years' sentence. A Russian plutocrat, Roman Abramovich, bought Chelsea football club.

The hot weather buckled railway lines in England and killed 3000 extra French people. The north-east of the USA and the whole of Italy were blacked out by power failures. Latvia voted to join the EU and Sweden voted not to join the Euro. In the Middle-East talks between President Bush, Ariel Sharon and Abu Mazen failed. The Liberian dictator Samuel Taylor was ousted. In Iraq Uday and Qusay Hussein were killed. Adult Iranian twin sisters joined at the head both died under an operation to separate them.

The BBC's Andrew Gilligan said that he had it on good authority that the government had 'sexed up' the dossier justifying the war on Iraq. The government's communications chief, Alastair Campbell, said that Gilligan had made it all up. The BBC backed its reporter. The row between the two institutions began to overshadow the question of whether the government had misled the nation.

2003

Dr David Kelly, who had been an arms inspector in Iraq, was identified as the source of the allegations in Andrew Gilligan's report. He appeared before the Foreign Affairs select committee on July 15. On July 18 he was found dead, having apparently committed suicide. Neither the government nor the BBC claimed any responsibility

WE'RE SORRY, BUT IT WAS THE OTHER LOT'S FAULT!

Monday **July 21**

2003

Lord Hutton, who led the inquiry into the events leading up to Dr Kelly's death, wanted to know how he had been identified as Andrew Gilligan's informant. He heard that at an MoD press conference they played a game in which journalists put up their guesses and the MoD indicated assent or dissent.

2003

Geoff Hoon, the defence secretary, seemed about to carry the can for exposing Dr Kelly to the media. As Labour prepared to go to Bournemouth for the annual conference his future certainly seemed uncertain.

Friday **September 26**

2003

The prime minister's future too was beginning to look less certain. However, he survived his party's attacks at the conference more or less intact and the family set off on holiday to stay with Cliff Richard in Barbados. His wife's odd relationship with Carole Caplin had recently added to his troubles, although she had saved his face by volunteering to sing "When I'm Sixty-Four" for some Beijing students.

2003

Thursday **July 31**

Military intelligence had believed that Saddam's relation and henchman Ali Hassan al Majid – "Chemical Ali" – was killed when his palace was attacked weeks ago. This proved not to be the case. Kurdish troops captured him and handed him over to the coalition.

Friday **August 22**

2003

The Iraq Survey Group, led by the CIA, had in six months' search come to believe less and less in Saddam's hidden weapons of mass destruction. In this case intelligence proved not to be misleading. The group reported to Congress that it had failed to find any trace of an arsenal.

2003   Thursday **September 25**

The government renounced its plan to close schools that had failed to reach improvement targets for three years running.

The Metropolitan police renounced their fruitless attempt to prove that Chief Superintendent Ali Dizaei was corrupt. He had been claiming that the force, even after good resolutions prompted by the MacPherson report, was institutionally racist. The failure to make the charges stick rather supported the chief superintendent's point.

2003

The Tories plotted successfully to oust Iain Duncan Smith, enthroning Michael Howard in his place. Chancellor Gordon Brown did not replace Tony Blair, despite the latter's many troubles and waning popularity. George Galloway was expelled from the party for indiscipline. President Bush made a bizarre State Visit almost entirely in private. Ken Livingstone was invited to rejoin the party. Delayed Northern Ireland elections produced victory for the more extreme elements on both sides, putting paid to the Good Friday Agreement.

Manchester United's Rio Ferdinand was fined and suspended for failing to take a drug test. David Beckham was sold to Real Madrid. England won the Rugby World Cup. Benjamin Zephaniah won applause for not accepting an OBE. Professor Colin Blakemore complained that he had not got one due to secret pressure from animal libbers. A conclave of Anglican archbishops failed to agree about gay priests and bishops. The royal family was shaken by ex-butler Paul Burrell's allegations of louche behaviour in the palace. Concorde was scrapped. Ian Huntley was found guilty of murdering Soham schoolgirls Holly Wells and Jessica Chapman. Police were blamed for not warning the school about his predilections.

Saddam Hussein was found in a primitive dugout near Tikrit. Colonel Gadafy made overtures to the West to come in from the cold. Edward Shevardnaze was peacefully ousted from the leadership in Georgia. Arnold Schwarzenegger was elected Governor of California. Poland and Germany fell out over the EU constitution. An earthquake devastated the ancient Iranian city of Bam killing 50,000 people.

On October 21 New Labour's founding spin-doctor celebrated a birthday, his fiftieth if you must know.

Wednesday **October 22**

Leeds University business school reported that British bailiffs were chasing £5 billion of personal debt, mostly run up on credit cards.

Gordon Brown was optimistic about the Treasury's debts. In his pre-budget statement he was confident that economic growth would allow the government to pay its bills without raising taxes.

2003 Thursday **December 11**

Tony Blair had excluded his rival Gordon Brown from Labour's national Executive Committee. They then tried to demonstrate to the public that they were still on good terms by announcing that they would have dinner together at Downing Street.

Friday **November 7**

2003

The Conservatives made no effort to hide their conflicts. MPs plotted openly to oust Iain Duncan Smith from the leadership. He retained some popularity with the wider party, however, and got a standing ovation at the conference.

2003

There was intense security for President Bush's state visit to Britain. Central London became a zero-tolerance zone. Only the Queen, Mr Blair and security staff actually got to see the president.

Her Majesty's own security was a lot less stringent. A Daily Mirror reporter got a footman's job at Buckingham Palace with ridiculous ease, using one false reference.

2003   Thursday **November 20**

The long smouldering dispute between fire-fighters and their local government employers threatened to flare up again over the way last June's agreement was being implemented. The public's early emotional support for the strikers had rather gone off the boil.

The publicity surrounding the Rugby World Cup aroused passionate enthusiasm for the bourgeois game of rugby union football. England's victory momentarily made it more popular in that country than proletarian soccer and its nouveau riche stars.

2003   Monday **November 24**

2004

January to May

2004

Lord Hutton's report found the government almost without fault in the death of Dr Kelly. The Chairman of the Governors and the Director General of the BBC resigned. Another judge, Lord Butler, was deputed to settle the question of unreliable intelligence but not the question of what the government did with it. This caused Michael Howard to withdraw the Tory Party's support. The mass murderer Dr Shipman hanged himself in prison. Lord Black lost his grip on the Daily Telegraph. Shell found that they had much less oil in reserve than they had thought. Eurotunnel fell into the inexperienced hands of indignant small shareholders. Marks and Spencer were struggling. The island was not at once swamped by tidal wave of eager immigrants when the new members joined the EU.

In Iraq outsiders joined the local resistance to US troops. Both sides killed many innocents. Photographs of American jailers gleefully torturing their Iraqi prisoners further hampered the battle for hearts and minds. Terrorists bombed commuters in Madrid and threatened to bomb BA flight 223, which was repeatedly cancelled. People suspected of terrorist intent were arrested in west London and north-west England. Republican and Loyalist extremists made big gains in Northern Ireland. Israeli helicopters assassinated Abdul Aziz Rantisi and Sheikh Yassin in his wheelchair. President Bush welcomed Ariel Sharon's plan to abandon Gaza in return for consolidating the Israeli presence on the West Bank. Colonel Gadafy of Libya renounced terrorism and blew the whistle on some former co-conspirators. North Korea and our Pakistani allies in the war against terrorism turned out to be the most enthusiastic traders in WMD.

There was controversy over the impending arrival of citizens of countries about to join the EU on May 1. The optimists pointed out that they would probably bring skills that are increasingly rare in this country.

2004

Thursday April 29

British xenophobes persuaded the government to promise to make it difficult for east Europeans newly admitted to the EU to come here as 'benefit tourists'.

Jean-Marie Le Pen, the cross-Channel xenophobe, addressed the political organisation most perfectly representing this tendency, the BNP, in a Manchester suburb.

The xenophobic tendency continued to get mixed messages. The Home Office announced that foreign workers would be welcome. At the same time the Department for Education announced that there was a shortage of mathematics teachers.

Tuesday **February 24**

2004

The immigration minister, Beverley Hughes, had failed to react to reports that Bulgarian and Romanian immigrants had been knowingly allowed in with bogus qualifications, perhaps only pretending to be mathematics teachers. The resulting outcry forced her to resign

2004

Friday **April 2**

Tony Blair was suffering from unprecedented unpopularity. Even the Archbishop of Canterbury excoriated him for misleading the public over the reasons for going to war with Iraq and for attempting to suppress criticism.

Lord Hutton was less hostile to the Prime Minister. His report on the circumstances leading to the death of Dr Kelly castigated the BBC and its Today programme. The government and its servants were almost entirely blameless. Downing Street's press secretary, Alastair Campbell, found himself occupying the moral high ground, overlooking the corporation.

2004   Thursday **January 29**

The host of BBC daytime TV chatshow, Robert Kilroy-Silk had written an article in the Sunday Express abusing Arabs in general. British prisoners in the US detention centre at Guantánamo Bay might have imagined that this point of view was endorsed by their government.

Some British Muslims still at home also appeared to take a dim view of the government. Police found a cache of fertiliser explosive, as used by the IRA, in a lock-up garage in suburban west London. They made dawn raids and arrested some young Muslim men.

2004

British Muslims were not the only group believing themselves to be persecuted by the government. Barristers, unhappy with the home secretary's new arrangements for paying them, threatened to withdraw their labour.

Friday **April 23**

2004

German shepherd dogs too might be excused for imagining themselves the victims of unfair prejudice. West Midlands police decided to abandon them in favour of Rottweilers because they had grown 'soft'.

2004

It was not only the government, it seemed, that held the BBC in low esteem. Some of the corporation's digital channels had ratings of zero as they were watched by fewer than a thousand people.

Tuesday **January 13**

2004

The BBC's digital broadcasts to a tiny audience might be construed as catering for an elite. The Royal Opera House did not want to have such a reputation. It will sell a few of its £175 seats for £10 in order to attract a less exclusive crowd.

2004

Wednesday **April 7**

June to September

2004

George Tenet of the CIA resigned, over the misuse of intelligence in selling the war to the American public. John Scarlett had performed the same service for his government but his elevation to head of MI6, went ahead unimpeded.

The government proposed ID cards to help fight terrorism but nobody seemed sure that they would be effective. Suspicion of the proposed EU constitution led to successes in the Euro elections for The UK Independence Party. The Barclay brothers bought the Telegraph. Philip Green failed to buy Marks and Spencer. Shell failed to satisfy the FSA that it had been thruthful about it's oil reserves. Sporting tradition was maintained as England went out of the Euro 2004 competition and Tim Henman went out of Wimbledon. The Football Association got into trouble trying to publicise the love affairs of the England coach, Sven Goran Eriksson.

The new Interim Government of Iraq put Saddam Hussein on trial. Coalition forces, in that government's name, fought the Mahdi Army of Moqtada al Sadr in Falluja. The fighting was punctuated by uneasy cease-fires. Hostage taking became a regular feature of life. Some was merely commercial but dissidents, mainly from outside the country, tried to detach member nations from the Coalition by issuing gruesome videos of the beheading of hostages. African forces attempted to stop killing of civilians in Darfur. John Kerry was chosen to oppose President Bush in the US election. Greece got the Olympic Games site ready by the skin of its teeth.

The United States aspired to bring American freedom to Iraq. Unfortunately they were caught bringing the conditions of the worst sort of American prison to Abu Ghraib jail in Baghdad. This did little to endear American democracy to the inmates.

2004

Tuesday **May 11**

Leaders of the Church of England quarrelled bitterly over the appointment of Canon Jeffrey John as bishop of Reading. The canon had declared himself to be gay; the liberal wing of the church considered this to be perfectly acceptable, the evangelicals thought the canon was bound for damnation.

Friday **June 18**

Another religious leader, Abu Hamza, the hook-handed, glass-eyed ex-imam of the Finsbury Park mosque, had upset the government. He was arrested and sent to Belmarsh prison as a result of an extradition request from the US. He may be there for some time as US secretary of state Ashcroft unwisely said that he would face the death penalty, thus blocking the extradition.

The photographs printed in the Daily Mirror, of British soldiers mistreating Iraqi prisoners, turned out to be fakes, as many had suspected. They had been mocked-up in the back of the wrong kind of lorry. The editor of the Mirror was sacked. The scandal drove the question of whether British soldiers had in fact tortured their captives from the front pages.

Friday **May 14**

2004

George Tenet also lost his job as head of the CIA over faulty information. The agency had been criticised for failing to predict the September 11 attack. The agency had also accepted mocked-up evidence that Saddam Hussein possessed weapons of mass destruction.

2004

Friday **June 4**

Opinion polls showed that Tony Blair's popularity had fallen to its lowest level ever. The public felt that he had accepted the unreliable evidence of the security services too readily. Lord Butler's report, however, had completely exonerated not only the prime minister but also the unreliable security services.

Tuesday **July 20**

2004

Robert Kilroy-Silk had, in contrast to the prime minister, remained popular with the public despite losing his daytime TV show and gaining a xenophobic reputation. In the event, this reputation worked to his advantage when he went campaigning for the UK Independence party in a Nottingham shopping mall.

2004

The government wanted to make smacking fractious children a criminal offence. Its plan to jail parents convicted of the assault drew charges of nanny-stateism. The Lords, many of whom had themselves been smacked by nannies and now employ nannies to do their smacking for them, voted to modify the bill to take into account the severity of the beating.

Tuesday **July 6**

2004

Tony Blair and Michael Howard both accepted that the state, though not our nanny, was obliged to care for us. They kicked off the election campaign by making promises about the NHS. As is now customary, both parties fought to occupy the same territory. Each leader said that his NHS would offer 'choice' but that his rival's was the wrong kind of choice.

2004

A man dressed as Batman appeared on a ledge on the facade of Buckingham palace. He claimed to represent Fathers 4 Justice, an organisation dedicated to getting fathers the right to see their children regularly. His partner revealed that she is leaving him because he failed to pay any attention to their child. All his time was spent demonstrating.

Wednesday **September 15**

2004

There was another incursion into the hallowed places of the state when three men representing the pro-foxhunting lobby burst into the Commons' chamber. They had quite easily evaded the security provided by men in tights. It was decided that the ceremonially dressed parliamentary officials must be replaced by something more modern.

2004   Friday **September 17**

English sporting patriots had been flaunting the cross of St George. Their enthusiasm was dimmed when England was ejected from the Euro 2004 competition in a humiliating penalty shoot-out after a less than brilliant match against the host nation. It was finally extinguished when Tim Henman fell to an undistinguished Serb in the Wimbledon quarter-final.

Thursday **July 1**

2004

Had the English team been successful in Euro 2004, the public might have been uncritical of sexual peccadilloes. In the prevailing atmosphere, when Mark Palios, chief executive of the Football association, tried to suppress reports of his affair with a fellow employee by giving the News of the World details of Sven-Goran Eriksson's affair with the same woman, he was forced to resign. Illogically, Sven's sexual adventures, rather than his coaching of the England team, were advanced as a reason for sacking him.

2004